Drawing for beginners:

Learn the Basics of Pencil Drawing in No Time (Sketching, Cool Stuff, Drawing Tips and Ideas)

I0488601

By Kirsten Little

CONTENTS

INTRODUCTION

Lots of people love to draw, but they have a strong belief that the drawing is a God gifted talent, and you can't learn it. Fortunately, you can learn drawing to make it a relaxing hobby. Different tips and suggestions are available for you to learn drawing. People want to learn to draw for various reasons, either for their passion of art or to get an additional talent.

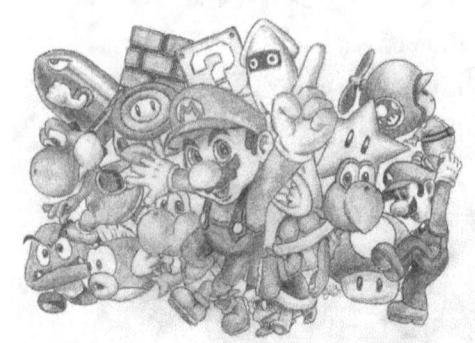

If you are interested to learn the drawing and sketching techniques, you can do it successfully because there are some techniques to learn, and with constant practice, you will be able to learn drawing. It is not difficult to learn because your constant practice is required to make you a master. Keep it in mind that it is not possible to become a master overnight; therefore, practice all drawing tutorials.

DRAWING MISTAKES BY BEGINNERS

A good drawing tutorial can help you to learn all basics of drawing, and you can easily remind all important things. If you want to learn drawing, it is important to arrange all important tools and accessories. Following are some drawing mistakes of beginners, and you should avoid them to bring perfection in your skills:

A HARD GRADE OF PENCIL

It is important to select the right pencil, such as if you are looking to draw shadows, the pencil should be pale. If you are using Number2HB pencil, then it will be hard for you to draw because of their light shading. You can try B, 2B and 4B for the darker values.

USE OF FLASH IN THE PORTRAIT PHOTOGRAPHY

Use of flash in the photographs is the major problem with the drawing of an apprentice. The blaze can crush the features of the photographs, and you will not be able to become more creative with it. You can highlight the features and skin tones of a face with the help of natural lighting.

HEAD PROPORTION

The facial features of a person can be drawn perfectly with the right head proportion. The problem may cause when you draw too big and squeeze the rest of the head.

FACIAL FEATURES, NOT ALIGNED

Typically, you look at a person in a point-blank range, and the people naturally try to make the features of the level. If you keep your head at an angle, you may find distorted results. You have to see the features from the same angle.

OUTLINE THE VALUE DRAWINGS

If you want to draw values, create an illusion of different tonal values. Any hard-drawn line can disrupt your illusion, and let the edge defined by the two different areas of the tonal value meeting.

SELECTION OF THE WRONG PAPER

Cheap papers have a shine on the surface, and it can be difficult to draw on this paper. You can use a thick notepad to have enough surface to draw a sketch. Use a firm surface under the sheet of paper because any uneven texture can make it difficult to draw different items.

USE PENCIL LINES TO DRAW HAIR AND GRASS

If you want to draw hair and grass, use a single pencil line to give a natural look. The feathery pencil strokes will help you to draw shades and dark foliage in the background of grass and hair.

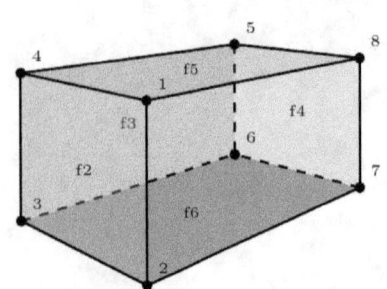

Sketching means freehand drawing, and the sketching is used for various purposes, such as to demonstrate an image and idea. Any drawing medium can be used to draw sketches, and the sketches are typically drawn to prepare a nicely finished work of art. The sketches are drawn with the help of quick marks, and the nuts and bolts of the drawing are worked out in every sketching stage of the artistic process. There should be a balance between the values and proportion.

MEDIUMS AND SURFACES FOR DRAWING

It is important to consider the medium, such as graphite, charcoal, ink and other mediums to create sketches. You can use pastels and colored pencils to draw sketches, but the surface is another medium to consider. You should select an appropriate area to distinguish sketches from drawings. Usually, lower quality papers are used to create sketches. The low-quality papers may be newsprint, but the highest quality papers are often used for drawing. There is no difference between sketching and drawing despite the medium used in the both arts

HOLDING THE PENCIL

There are different myths about an artist to hold a pencil, but the artificial grip on the pencil will make your drawing worse. It can be the reason of stress and upset the natural flow of your drawing. Basically, the tripod grip is required to hold a pencil while drawing.

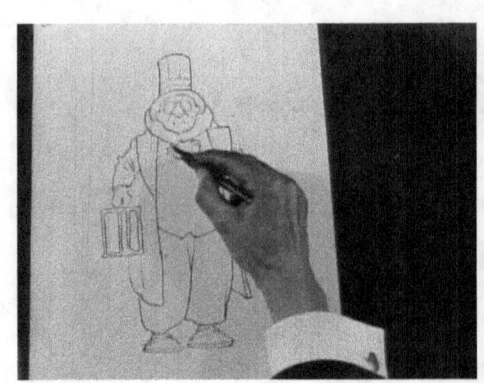

The tripod grip is quite similar to your grip you used in writing. The thumb and the forefinger form a triangle on the pencil with the middle finger. You can give support of ring finger and pinkie as well. The grip helps you to hold the pencil in an ideal way to draw all fine details. The upright position of the pencil helps you to share the drawing with the tip instead of using the side of the pencil.

TRIPOD GRIP

You can give support of your fingers and thumb to the tripod grip while holding a pencil. It will help you to draw fine images, and if you want to avoid smudges and oils of the skin, you can use a spare sheet. You can use the wrist or elbow to support additional movements on the drawing surface.

EXTEND TRIPOD GRIP

You can extend the tripod grip to hold the pencil in a useful way because the grip will help you to draw in a comfortable way. The tripod grip will be formed in the similar way, and it gives you the freedom to try different movements of fingers and hand. In the extended grip, you will be able to create larger movements of the pencil tip with small movements. It is an efficient way to grip the pencil for better results in sketching. A relaxed grip can give you better results as compared to a tight and vicelike grip.

FROM THE OVERHAND GRIP

The overhand grip is used for sketching because it helps you to use the side of the pencil while sketching. The overhand grip enables you brace the pencil lightly against your fingers while keeping your thumb straight. The position of the pencil may vary based on the proportions of your hand, but you have to keep your grip relaxed on the pencil.

UNDERHAND PENCIL GRIP

It is a loose and relaxed grip in which you have to form a tipped-over tripod grip. It enables you to keep your thumb higher and let the pencil, sit in the V shape formed between the thumb and palm. The index and middle finger may lightly control the pencil. The grip is useful for the casual broad sketching with the help of charcoal pencil.

STRUCTURAL SKETCHES

It is a type of engineering design of the buildings and other structures required to build. The registered personnel are often hired to make the structural drawings. The structural designs outline the size and type of material will be used in the construction. These are designed to address the architectural details that are finishes, surface and partition walls. The structural drawings often communicate the structure and design of the building to the reviewing authority. The designs are an important part of the contract documents because these provide guidance for detailing, fabrication and installing parts.

BLACK AND WHITE SKETCHES

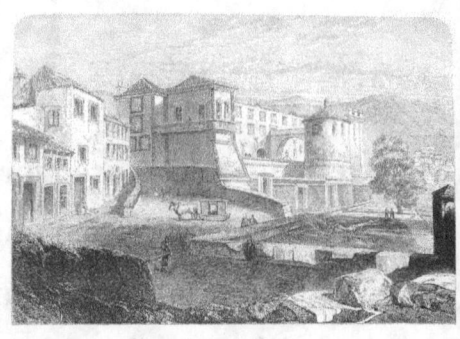

Black and white sketches are really attractive for lots of people because these are based on the pencil drawing. If you are interested to learn how to draw, then you can use a pencil as a main medium because it will give you a solid base to start your learning process. The black and white sketches have their own importance and demands as compared to the color pictures. You can use crayons, sketch pencils, and charcoal to design black and white sketches. It will be quite interesting to learn black and white sketches to draw different figures, such as face, bird, animal, hair and different other items to enhance their features.

COLOR SKETCHES

The color sketches are important in different walks of life, specifically in the fashion designing. If you want to be the part of fashion or film industry, you should learn the color sketches. Different colors are used to enhance the features of an item. It is also necessary for the architecture, web designing,

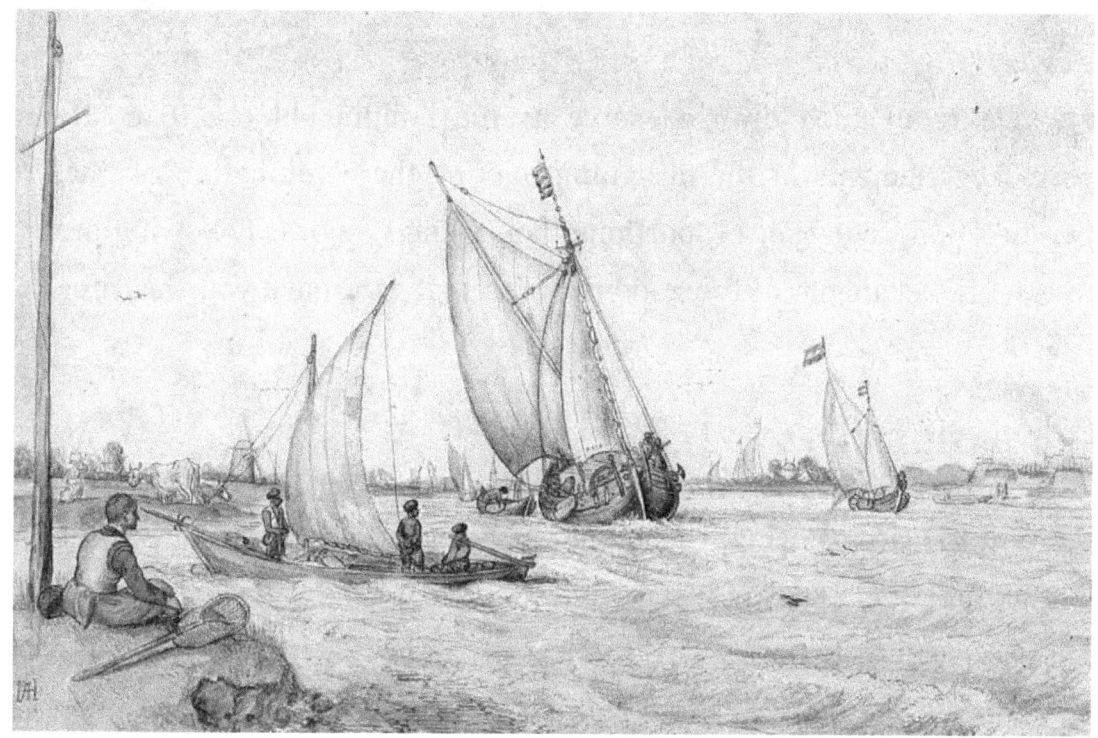

and production department.

CHAPTER 02: ELEMENTS OF GOOD DRAWING (USE OF BASIC SHAPES, GAUGING PROPORTIONS, MEASURING ANGLES, USE OF REFERENCE MATERIAL, LINEAR PERSPECTIVE, VANISHING POINTS, ATMOSPHERIC PERSPECTIVE)

The principles of good drawing serve as the building blocks to create artwork. The elements of the designing may be the combination of line, shape, direction, material, proportions, points, and angles. Following are some essential elements of the good drawing that can make your learning easy:

USE OF BASIC SHAPES

If you want to learn drawing, you should have a good understanding of the basic shapes of drawing. Any sketch or design is usually comprised of the basic shapes. The basic shapes of drawing are:

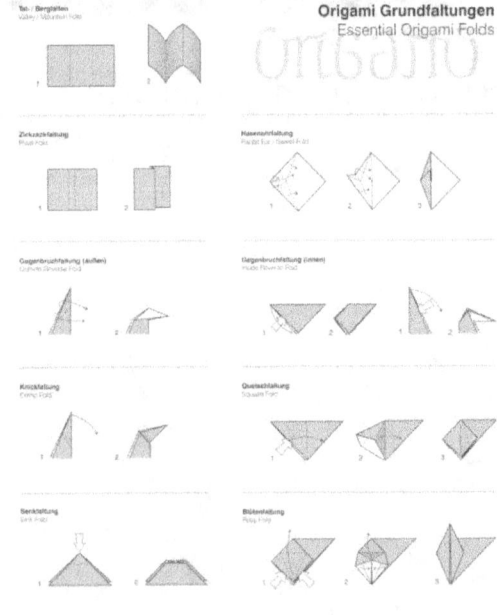

- Lines
- Arrows
- Rectangles and squares
- Ellipses and circles
- Curves and polygons
- Connectors

Line and arrows: A line in the drawing is measured by the length and it is often used to separate two objects. The lines are used in the drawing as separating line, shadow line, hatching, negative space, representative lines and grouped objects. If the line is drawn for the pointing purpose, then the arrows are used on either or both heads of the lines. The lines and arrows are also known as connectors to join two objects with each other.

RECTANGLES AND SQUARES:

Rectangles and squares are designed with round or square edges in the pencil drawing to draw different shapes, such as a wall, room, building, etc. You can use T-square drawing tool to make your work easy.

ELLIPSES AND CIRCLES

Ellipse is a curve on a plane adjacent to two focal points and it can be perfectly designed with the help of drawing pins. The circle is a geometric shape with equal distance from any of the points and the center. The shape of the circle is quite relevant to curve. In the drawing, the ellipses and circles prove helpful to draw the human body or any animal.

CURVES AND POLYGONS

Curves and polygons are different geometrical notions that help you to design various objects. The curves and polygons are specifically important to design charts, graphs and other shapes used to present financial data or growth of an organization. These shapes are frequently used in the drawing.

GAUGING PROPORTIONS

It means you have to measure the width and height of the object while drawing different objects. If you want to draw appropriately, you should learn to gauge the proportions accurately. There is no need to know the inches and centimeters, but you can measure the relative sizes of the elements. You can gauge the portions with the help of various tools from pencil to sewing gauges or dividers. With the help of a pencil, you can gauge the objects by keeping it close to the object and place your thumb at the end to compare this measurement with other parts. The gauging proportions are comparatively easy with the help of other tools, including sewing gauges.

MEASURING ANGLES

The angles are measured with the help of a tool known as the protector. The red and black crossbars are available along the vertex. The vertex indicates the point where the two rays of an angle meet with each other. You can also use a scale to measure the angles of a drawing shape. You can also use a pencil to measure the angles because it is a handy way to quickly complete your work.

USE OF REFERENCE MATERIAL

You can use reference materials (art books, photographs, magazines) to get some help. In order to have an idea of your work, you can use lighter reference lines for the features of the human face, body or other shapes. With the help of reference lines, you can draw a line to specify a particular value in the view.

LINEAR PERSPECTIVE

Linear perspective is a useful technique in the drawing for the representation of three-dimensional images. The linear perspective deals with the organization of shapes in space and the aerial perspective deals with the atmospheric effects on the tones and colors.

VANISHING POINTS

It is a point in which the things get further away from you and they seem smaller and closer to each other. As soon as they go far enough away, the distance becomes thinner and converted to a single point. The vanishing points have different perspectives, including:

- One-point perspective
- Two-point perspective
- Constructing perspective
- Atmospheric Perspective

It refers to the effects of the atmosphere on the appearance of an object to view it from a distance point. It is also known as aerial perspective and frequently used for sunrise and sunset. The saturation of the colors can be less as compared to the background colors. A decreasing trend is used in the contrast of the background and the object.

CHAPTER 03: DRAWING SUPPLIES AND TECHNIQUES FOR BEGINNERS

If you want to learn pencil drawing, it is important to arrange all important materials, tools and supplies.

QUALITY DRAWING PENCILS

Your drawing will be incomplete without the quality drawing pencils, and the pencil sets are available in packages. Some pencil set has harder graphite 9H pencils and 6B softer graphite pencils. The harder graphite pencils are used to make lighter marks. You have to use the sharp tip of a pencil. If you want to make darker marks, you can opt for the softer graphite. Make sure to resharpen the pencil again and again. The drawing pencil set will help you to increase your ability to work with different values. You can also get individual pencils, for instance, 2H, HB, 2B and 4B pencils.

SKETCHBOOK

The sketchbook is really important thing for an artist. It will help you to exercise different drawing images and sketches. It is a book or pad with blank pages frequently used by the artists to draw or paint. The sketchbooks are available in a variety of shapes and sizes with a variety of pages.

QUALITY DRAWING SURFACES

A variety of surfaces are available to draw, but you should choose the quality drawing surface. It is an important medium to select and following are some considerations for the selection of drawing surfaces:

THE TOOTH

A paper tooth is a surface texture used for pencil and pen drawing. The drawing papers with tooth are often sold as charcoal and pastel papers. Most of the painters prefer to use the drawing paper with heavy tooth. The smooth paper with less tooth is sold as a pen or pencil paper.

PAPER WEIGHT

The weight of the paper refers to the weight of each dream of the paper. A dream may contain 500 sheets, ad typically, the weight of the paper is directly linked to the thickness of the paper. Some thinner paper may have a heavy weight, for instance, the 80 lbs paper can be thicker than the 60 lbs paper.

ACID FREE

The acid-free paper has no yellow color and features more resistance to the fading colors. The paper has more resistance to UV light. You can experiment with the:

- Drawing paper with medium tooth
- Charcoal paper with a heavier tooth
- Bristol paper with smooth tooth

VARIETY OF ERASERS

Erasers are important to use for mistakes; therefore, it is a great tool to bring perfection to your drawing. Following are few types of erasers:

- Rubber Eraser: It is a standard eraser used to erase the graphite. The erasers use friction to remove the faults from the surface.
- Kneaded Eraser: It is a special eraser used to lift material from the surface. It can be used in different ways to create specific marks. The eraser will become dirty with consistent use, but you can knead it again.
- Gum Eraser: It is perfect to remove the media from the surface of the sensitive material. It can remove with the help of friction.
- Vinyl or Plastic Eraser: It is a toughest eraser to erase almost everything. It can tear the paper so it should be used very carefully.

GOOD PENCIL SHARPENER

The pencil is required to sharpen again and again. You have to use a good quality sharpener because a poor quality sharpener can spoil your drawing. There are two types of sharpener, handheld and stimulating:

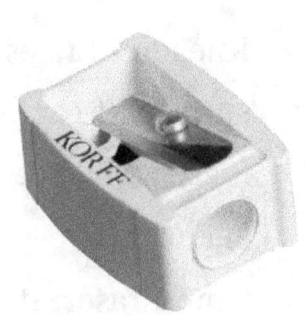

Electric Pencil Sharpeners: The electric pencil sharpener is available to sharp quickly, but you should not use it for color pencils. The waxy binder of the colored pencil can ruin the blades of the device.

Manual Pencil Sharpener: It is an appealing choice because most of the people prefer to use this sharpener. It is a simple and handheld sharpener available at cheap price. It is a cheap and portable solution.

CHARCOAL

The charcoal is important for black and white drawing because it can give a broader aspect and value to your drawing. It is available in both stick and pencil form. The stick charcoals are softened and produce lighter marks. The compressed charcoals are to produce darker marks. The pencil charcoals can be sharpened just like graphite pencils. Conte is quite similar to charcoal, but available in different colors.

FELT TIP PEN

A felt tip pen is absolutely important because it helps an artist to create a variety of marks. It enables you to design different things, and it has a good effect on the psychology of the artist. It can improve your drawing skills.

BLENDING STUMPS

The blending stumps are important for an artist who wants to smudge the colors or move the materials on the drawing surface. The blending stump enables an artist to create gradations without touching the oil and colors with your finger.

ARTWORK STORAGE

The storage of artwork is important to design your own portfolio. If you want to add your collection to your portfolio, it is important to store the artwork properly. You have to choose rigid portfolio to bend your art work at one place. The portfolio should have enough space to store your work.

STORAGE FOR ART MATERIAL

Just like your artwork, it is important to take care of your art material. You should find a suitable storage for your art material. You can buy a portable container with sufficient space to have all the items. Large variety of semi-portable containers and permanent stacks are available to carry art materials. You can choose any one storage bag based on your tools and art utilities.

CHAPTER 04: TIPS FOR PENCIL DRAWING SHADING AND COMPOSITION TECHNIQUES (IMPORTANT EXERCISES)

If you are looking to learn different drawing and shading techniques, buy some good quality drawing pencils and try following exercises:

EXERCISE FOR SHADING:

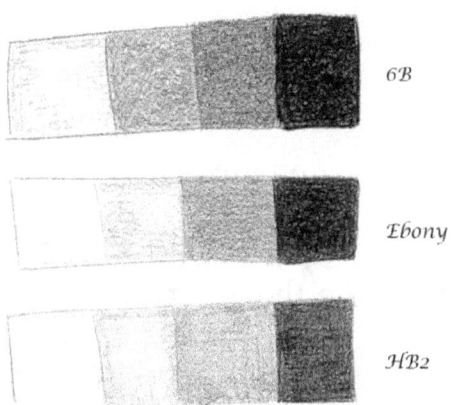

6B

Ebony

HB2

- Make a rectangle and divide it into four squares to use different pencils in each rectangle.
- Shade the first square oby holding the pencil in the middle and press lightly to get better effects.
- Shade the last square as dark as you can according to the capacity of your pencil. You can do layer over layer.
- The middle two squares can be shaded between lighter and darker values. You can use 2H pencil to expand your horizon.

EXERCISE FOR LINE

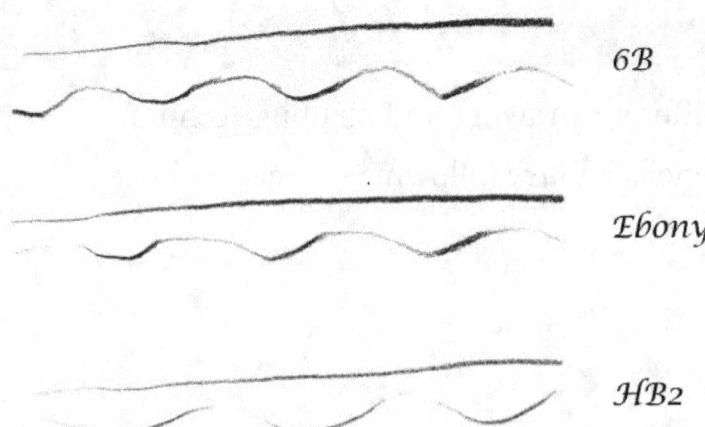

6B

Ebony

HB2

- You can draw a continuous line with your pencil, and start from light pressure and continuously increase the pressure on the pencil.

- Try to draw the line as dark as possible within the limitation of your tool. Repeat this with each pencil and focus on the potential of each one.

- Draw a straight line in the similar way, but start with the point of the pencil at the light end of the new line. Slowly increase the pressure on your pencil and use the side of the pencil for a broader and darker line.

- You can also try a wavy line from deep down to a thinner one, such as point of the wave should be thinner, and the top can be thicker.

- Repeat the exercise as many times as you become perfect to do it smoothly. Thickness and density of the line may be used for the indentations and overlapping.

HATCHING AND CROSS-HATCHING

You can draw a series of lines by placing them closely next to each other. You can create the value of a broader area, and the direction of the lines can be based on your choice and technique. You can overlap the series of parallel lines to create a dense value.

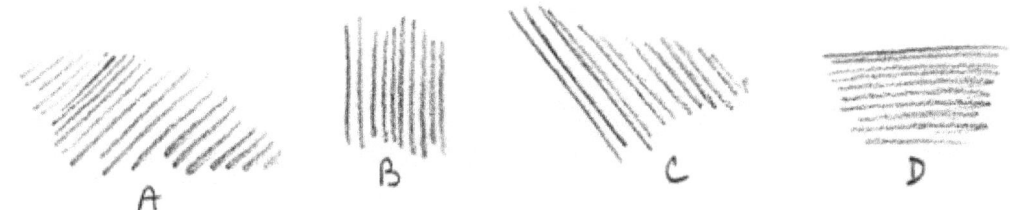

You can try these lines on your full sheet of paper and start with the different directions shown on the page. After practicing these lines for sufficient time, you can start overlapping these lines on a full sheet of paper.

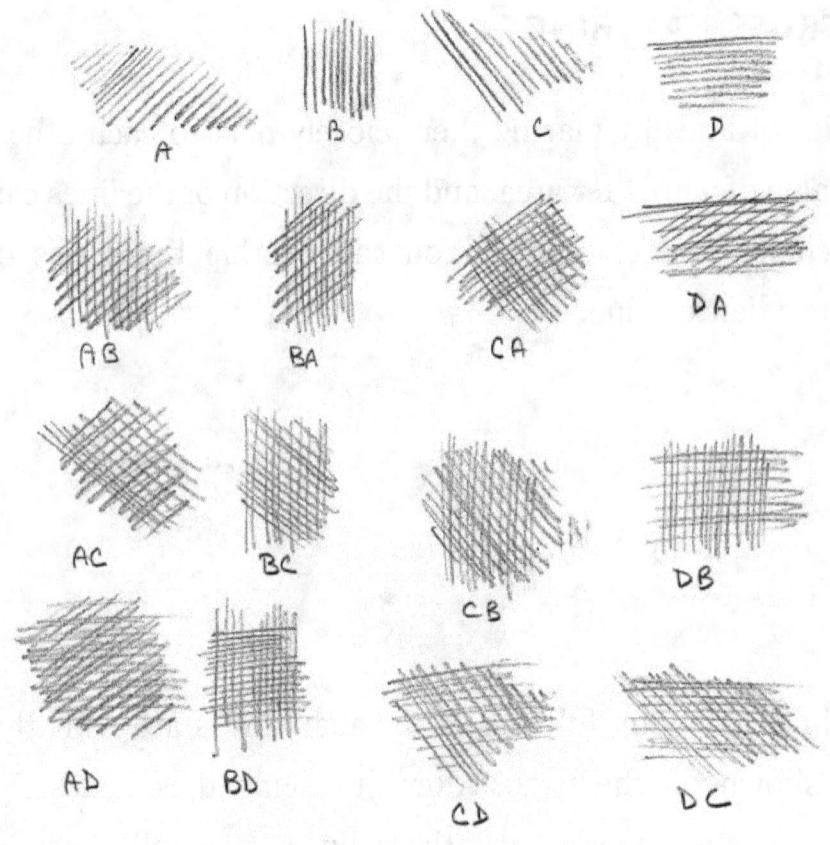

NON-PARALLEL HATCHING

It is not necessary that the hatching is parallel only, but it can be non-parallel also. You can taper off the density of the pencil from thicker to lighter lines.

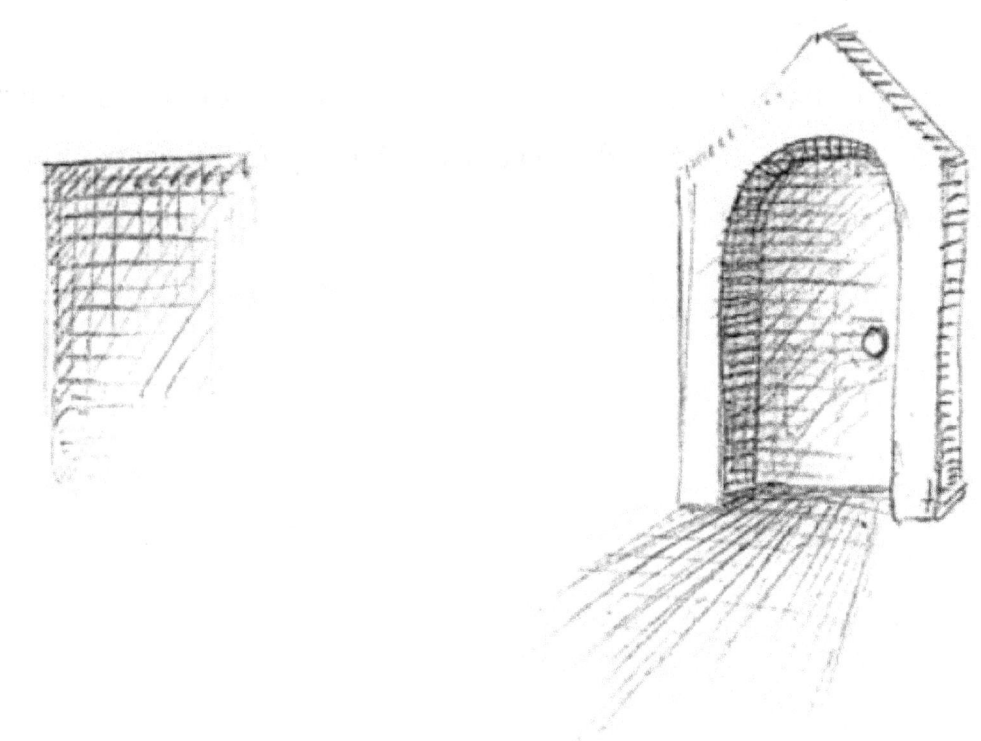

Hatching can be done for the textures and planes, and you can make different bricks with darker and lighter shades and hatching. The hatching is also done for volume with the two hexagonal prisms. Contour hatching is used for the rounded figures. You can build the illusion of hatching on the round shapes.

SCUMBLING AND STIPPLING

It is different from hatching because there is no need to follow direction. The techniques are used to avoid sharp edges. It helps you to design clouds, smoke, bushes and other items from a distance. You can exercise following image on your sketchbook:

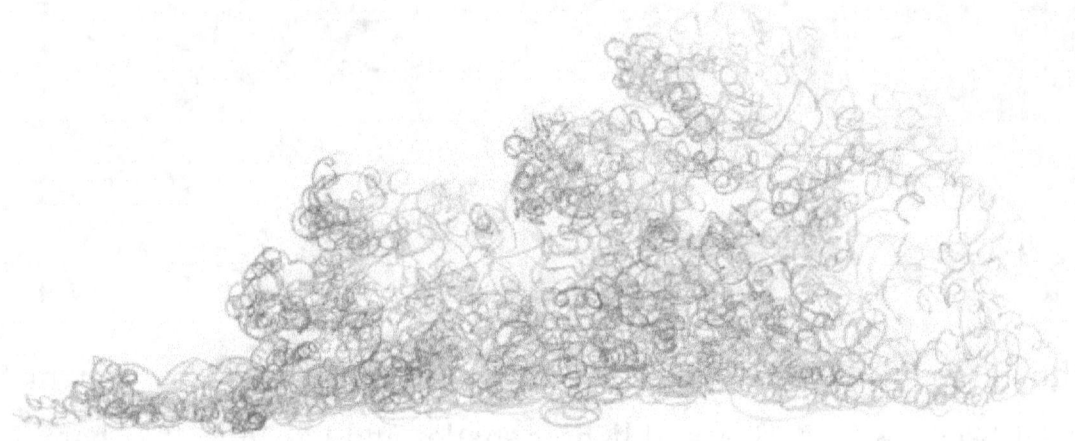

The stippling is done with the use of dots and small spots. The following image will help you to exercise:

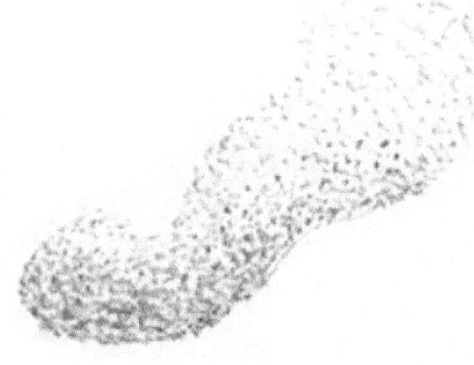

OTHER IMPORTANT VARIATIONS IN THE STROKE:

You can discover the use of the latest variations of the stroke to design trees with their own personality. The main goal of the drawing is to capture the movement and shapes in both negative and positive ways. You can blur the shades and draw each leaf. You can select any style according to your desires:

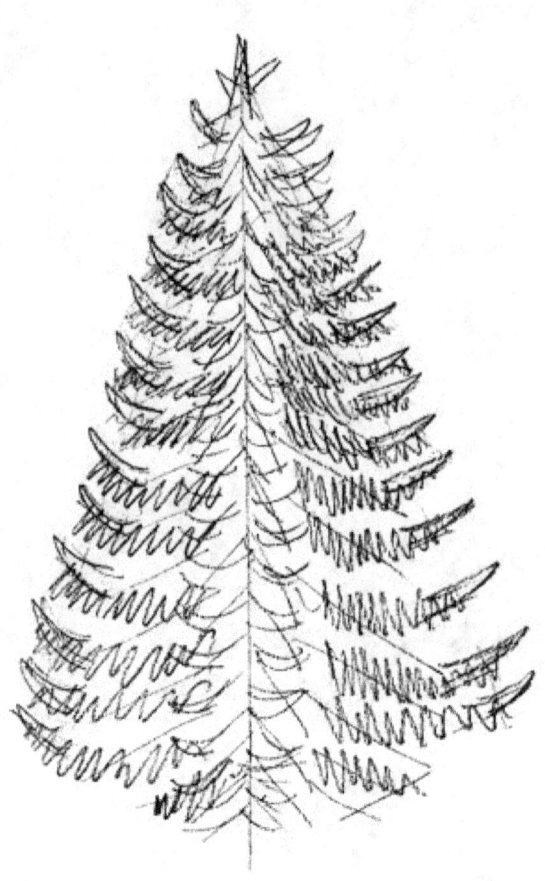

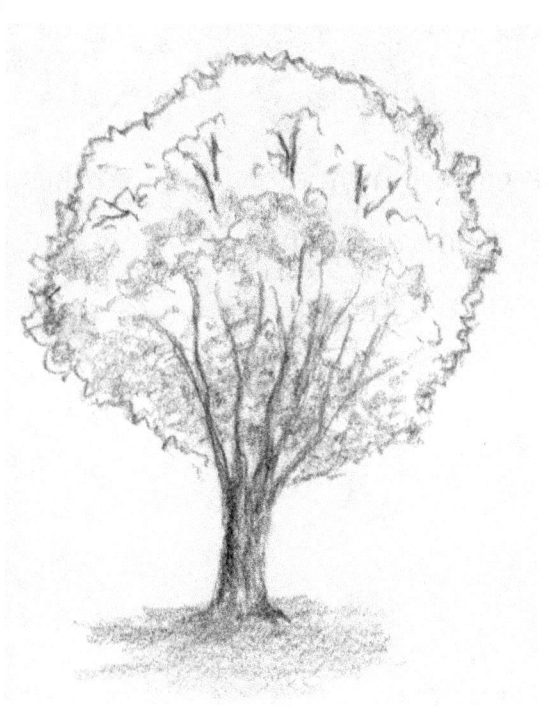

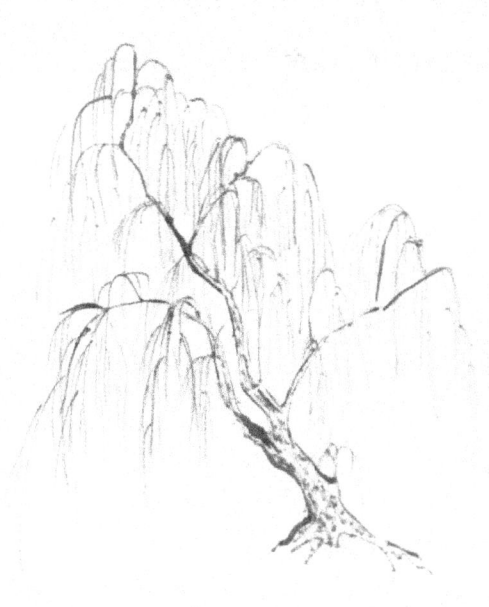

STROKES FOR ROCKS

The rocks are different in nature, and you can try from directional strokes to relatively smooth strokes. You have to represent bumpy, scraggly and uneven areas.

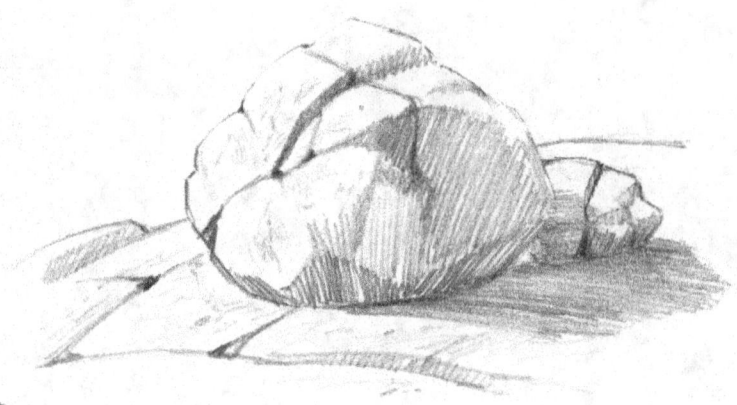

You can follow these strokes or try any other styles to design rocks in the drawing. Repeat all exercises as many times important to become an expert in this field.

The drawing tutorials look really interesting and easy, but without practice, you can't become a master. Following are some simple practices to try pencil sketching. You can try these sketches in your drawing book as many times as possible:

STILL LIFE

Still life is a picture, painting or photo of an object or a group of objects arranged together. A still life can be a tree, glass, flowers in the vase, old shoe, pile of toys, etc. If you want to draw a flower, practice following image in your sketching book:

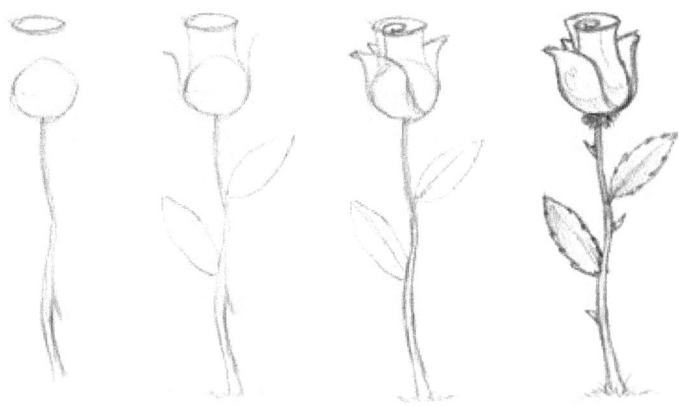

PRACTICE THE TREE ON YOUR DRAWING BOOK

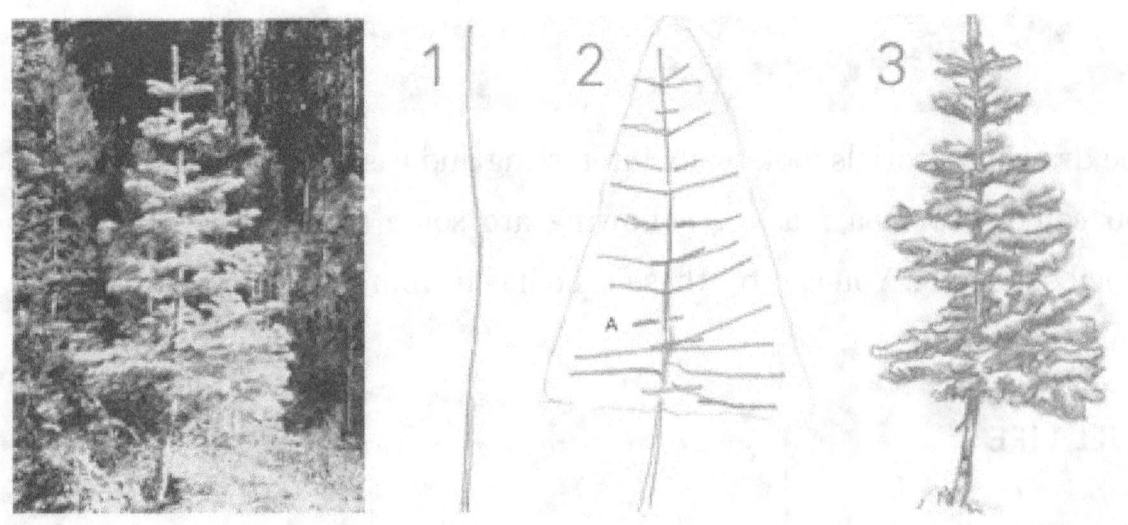

DRAW AN UMBRELLA WITH FOLLOWING SKETCHES

With the help of given below image, it will be really easy for you to draw an umbrella:

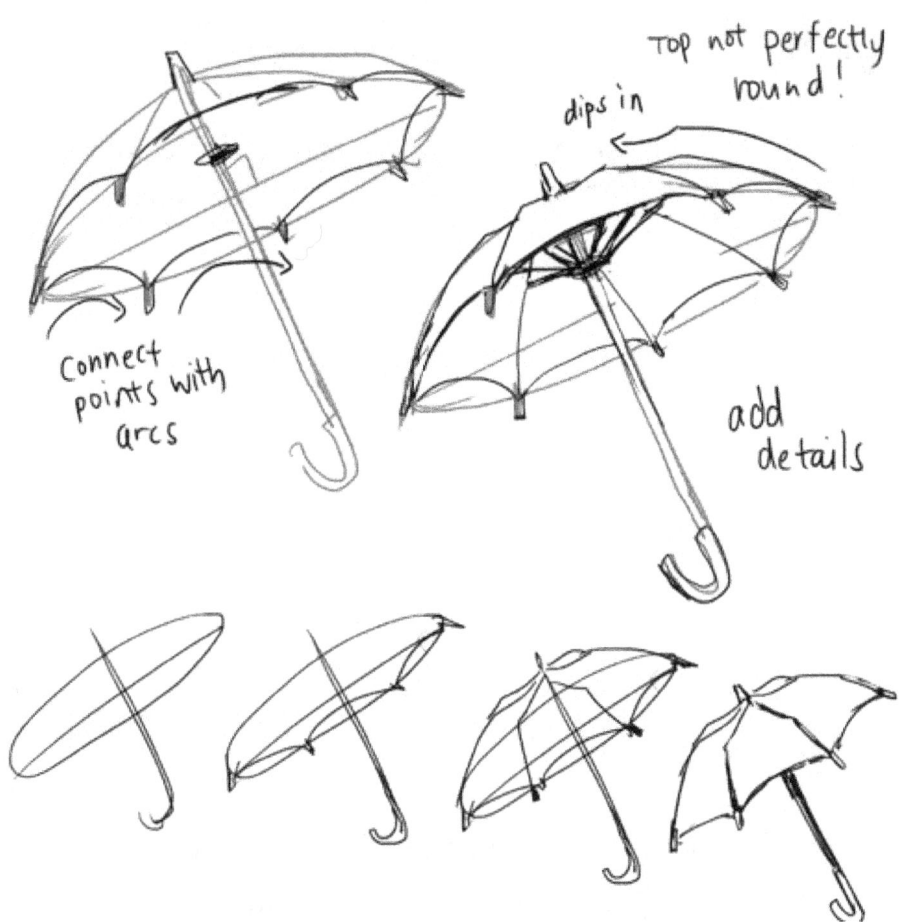

Top not perfectly round!

dips in

Connect points with arcs

add details

TEXTURED METAL

You can draw structural metal with different geometric forms because the metal surfaces require special attention. It is important to focus on the shades, lights, and highlights. Each and every detailing requires your complete focus and attention. You can make several sketches of the metal objects, glossy metal, and brushed items.

DRAW A COFFEE POT

If you want to draw a coffee pot, start drawing by constructing following simple geometric shapes:

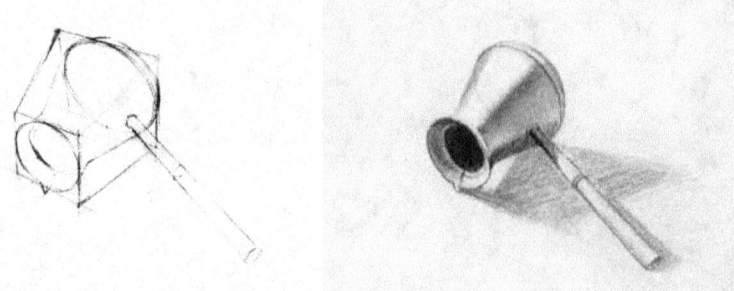

PERSPECTIVE SCENE

The perspective design is an important perspective techniques used to illustrate dimensions through a flat surface. There are various forms that will help you to draw different images and perspective from one perspective to two and three perspectives. There is a tutorial that will help you to draw a scene under a checkered pathway. You have to draw lines parallel to each other while considering vanishing points:

Start your work by creating a vanishing points at the center of the page, and to make your work easy, you can draw an "X" at the center. It will help you to draw lines at the edges of the paper you should draw lines to support another drawing.

In the next step, you have to draw a series of poles on the one side of the paper. Try to reach the vanishing point to alternate the poles with the series fo line.

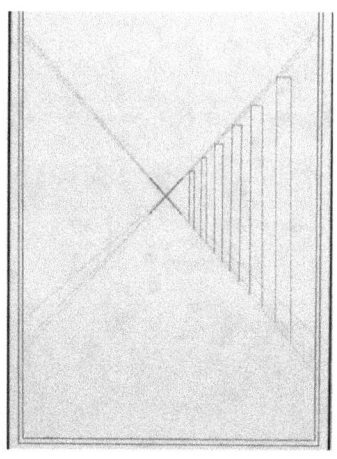

Now draw a series of pools on the other side, but it is important to draw some upright benches. You have to make sure that the lines should approach the center and vanishing point.

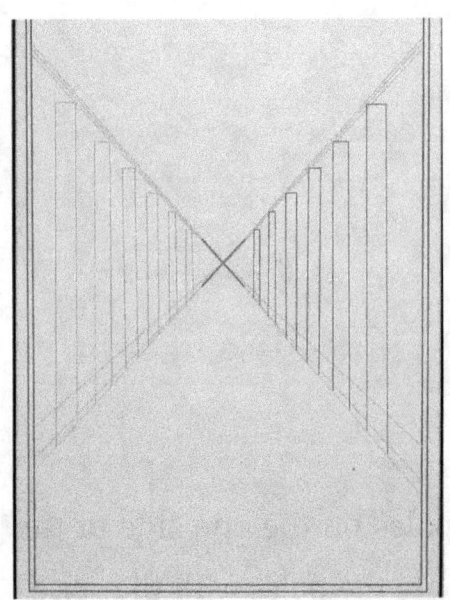

Draw the roof of the pathway by demonstrating its plaid pattern, and the following image will guide you through the process:

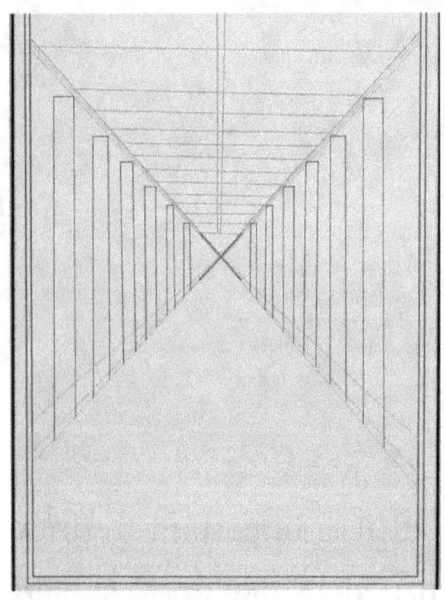

You can sketch different images on the left side, such as houses and a seaside or beach scene on the right side.

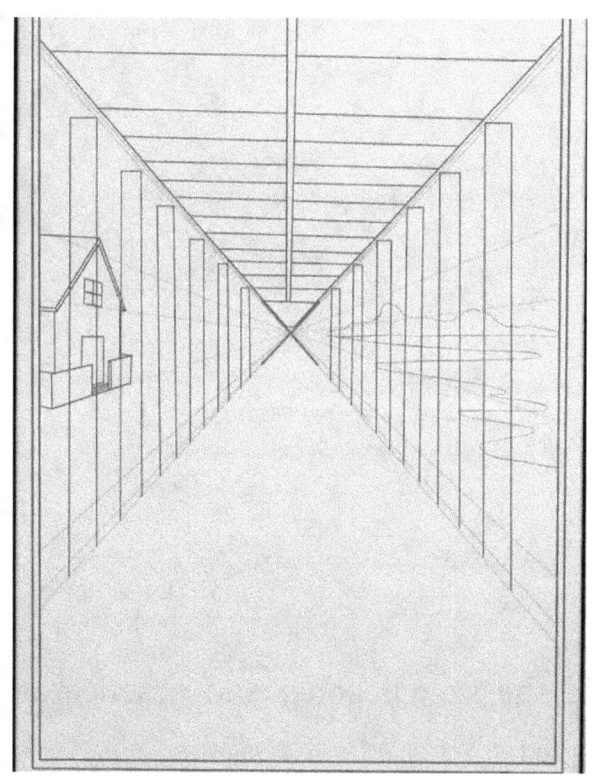

Highlight the sketching lines and highlight the paths and the roofs in the sketch. Ink over the design after completing it. You can use a black marker with different points, but you can make some variations in the texture of the design.

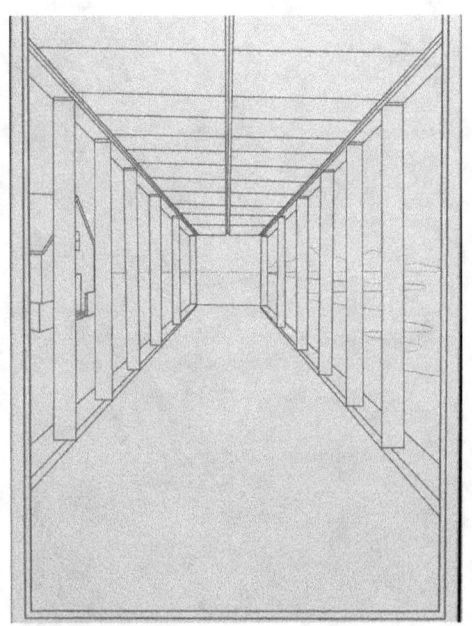

You can try above-mentioned steps in the sketch book, and practice as many times as you can to become an expert.

NATURAL SCENES

In the first step, you have to select a landscape to draw by simply selecting an image, look at its pictures and draw what you notice first. In the given image, you may notice the tree first, so draw the tree lightly, but give an outline only instead of details.

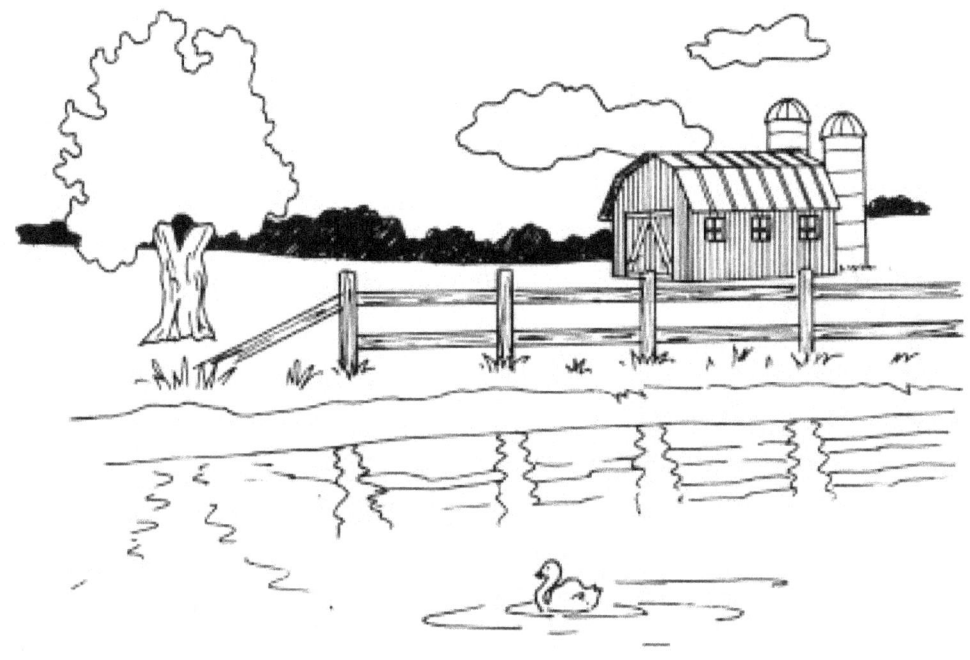

Start adding other details, such as rocks, river, grass, frames, and the hut, river, clouds, duck and shade them appropriately. You can use fingers to smooth the shades, or can use a pencil only to give a neat look to your sketch.

Finish your landscape by using colors for the hut, tree, water, duck and clouds. You can give light and dark touch-ups to your landscape. You can add different detailing to the landscape and the background to enhance the features of your drawing.

DRAW ANIMAL SKETCHES

Draw Animal Sketches

It is quite interesting to draw different sketches of animals with the help of spheres, four-sided figures, ellipse and other basic drawing shapes

DRAW ELEPHANT

The elephants are the biggest animals, and these have big ears, long trunk, and tusks. It will be quite interesting to draw an animal. There is no need to explain anything because following image will help you to draw an elephant. Practice it as much as you can to become an expert:

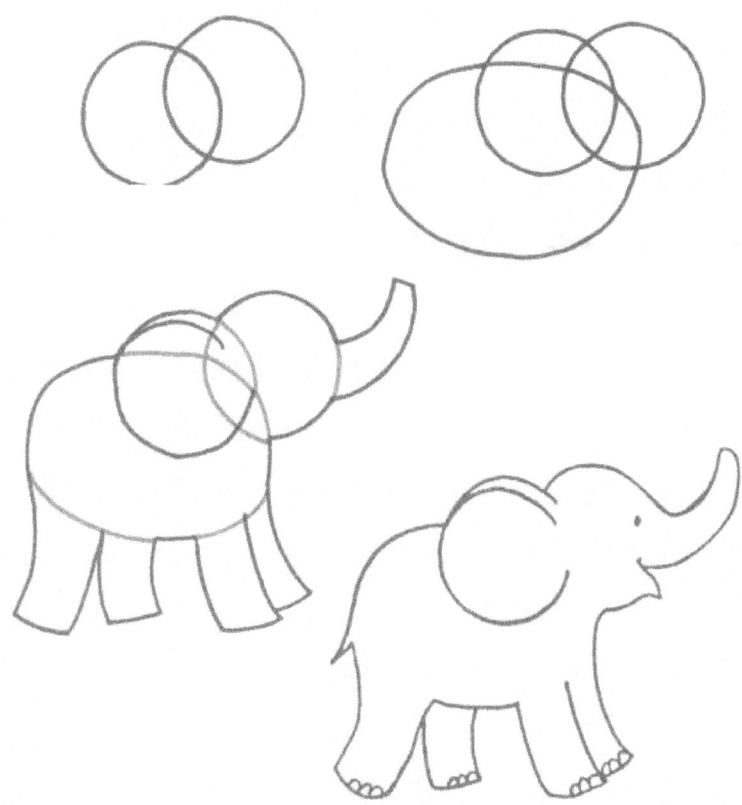

A Simple image is given below to make it easy for you to draw the sketches of a tweety:

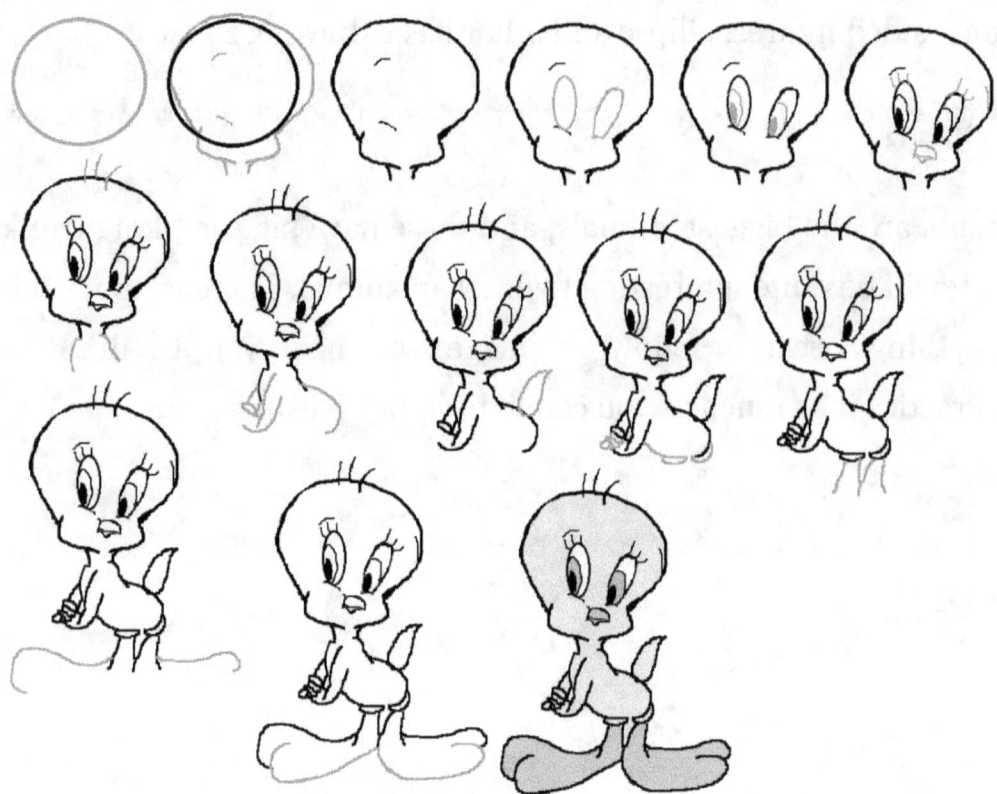

DRAW A HUMAN FACE

It is quite interesting to draw a human face because you have to consider lots of detailing, but it can be really simple with the help of following image:

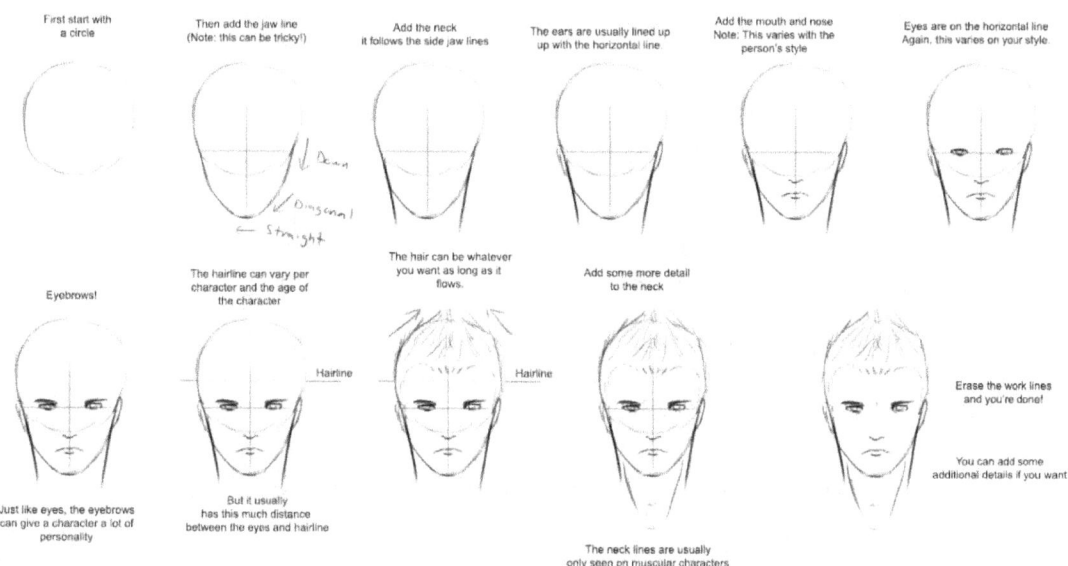

Practice all images as many times as you want because the practice makes a man perfect.

CONCLUSION

Drawing is a useful talent because you can make it a hobby or a source of earning. The people have the misconception that drawing skills are God gifted, but you can become an expert by practicing basic drawing structures again and again. If you want to learn drawing, it is important to arrange all important tools and accessories. You should know the types of pencils, erasers, sharpeners and other important tools to make your work easy. There are some simple tutorials that will guide you through step by step procedure. You should have a drawing book, and practice all images again and again to increase your expertise. There are some drawing principles that are important to know to make your practice easy.

You can use reference material, but practice is everything. If you want to become a professional drawing artist, you have to focus on each and every tutorial, practice every shape and try different combinations. You can design landscape scathes, animal faces, human face, natural scenes, flowers and much more by practicing basic things. For a beginner, it is important to start by drawing lines, shapes and hatching. Buy all important tools and practice drawing shapes on your art book as much as possible. It will be a great point for you to become an expert in this field. Regular practice will lead you to success; therefore, read this book and try all tutorials given in it to draw smoothly without any aid.

www.ingramcontent.com/pod-product-compliance
Lightning Source LLC
Chambersburg PA
CBHW081623170526
45166CB00009B/3087